BRAT

by Sophie Crocker

Guelph, Ontario

Edited by Shane Neilson
Cover and book design by Jeremy Luke Hill
Cover image by Brutus O'Gorman
Proofreading by Carol Dilworth
Set in Linux Libertine
Printed on Mohawk Via Felt
Printed and bound by Arkay Design & Print

LIBRARY AND ARCHIVES CANADA CATALOGUING IN PUBLICATION

Title: Brat / by Sophie Crocker.
Names: Crocker, Sophie, author.
Description: Poems.
Identifiers: Canadiana (print) 20220246963 | Canadiana (ebook) 20220246998 |
    ISBN 9781774220641 (softcover) | ISBN 9781774220658 (PDF) |
    ISBN 9781774220665 (HTML)
Classification: LCC PS8605.R625 B73 2022 | DDC C811/.6—dc23

ONTARIO ARTS COUNCIL
CONSEIL DES ARTS DE L'ONTARIO
an Ontario government agency
un organisme du gouvernement de l'Ontario

Gordon Hill Press gratefully acknowledges the support of the Ontario Arts Council.

Gordon Hill Press respectfully acknowledges the ancestral homelands of the Attawandaron, Anishinaabe, Haudenosaunee, and Métis Peoples, and recognizes that we are situated on Treaty 3 territory, the traditional territory of Mississaugas of the Credit First Nation.

Gordon Hill Press also recognizes and supports the diverse persons who make up its community, regardless of race, age, culture, ability, ethnicity, nationality, gender identity and expression, sexual orientation, marital status, religious affiliation, and socioeconomic status.

Gordon Hill Press
130 Dublin Street North
Guelph, Ontario, Canada
N1H 4N4
www.gordonhillpress.com

for my loves

Table of Contents

"I couldn't get the boy to kill me, but I wore his jacket for the longest time."
　　　— Richard Siken

"Thanks. I cannot be ruined."
　　　— Aisha Sasha John

venus in cancer

about me: i am a last resort. i tried to be anyone else first.

i think about dying the same way i think about dinosaurs. how difficult to dig out from the core of the earth with only a fork.

as a prank i would ask for Lean Cuisine on death row. let the guards myth me to their wives.

everything that feels good makes me want to vomit. rollercoaster or thumb on the tongue. every breath a bulimia of the lungs.

lately i am having an excellent time with my breasts. the heads of baby dolls that photosynthesize when my top comes off. spirals, meeting at the center of who i am.

anything worth having is worth having twice.

there is so much left to look up. approximate number of seashells on a beach? how much do hedgehogs sleep?

once, in a dark theatre, i sucked a sweetheart's finger so long i came out parasitic. once, i wore lipstick & cowboy boots to a funeral, neckline so low i'd seem a bluebell from above.

on the excoriation of Adam: i too would reel youth from my chest if this rendered my navel inexplicable.

of course, i've thought a lot about my last meal. it would be simple mutilated sunflowers, string cheese, prosecco from a bucket with a hole in the bottom. i don't want to miss anything before i have to. i can't even finish a podcast, can't even keep a middle name.

i once heard an oil baron say, *in a drought, it's more hope than water that's missing.* i've tried to drink hope – from the shallows of my favourite lover's throat – & came away dry.

probably i was born so someone new could speak a pun about loneliness. probably i was born to form a confetto of dismemberment.

when i look at the moon i think, *what an unwelcome miracle.* who asked for tides, blood once a month, a great blonde widow begging for light.

actually, my last meal will be breakfast.
                after breakfast i will take a long,
                        long walk.

we have to launder the sunflowers!

everyone is someone else's tadpole! at least, i can't breathe air yet
please teach me amphibiousness!

i can diagonal to any coordinate!

circumcise a rainbow! that's how you get your gold, love! hold
your thumb over the sun

love is only a horizon
what happens after! at the edge of the field
a forest, a mountain, a planet in heat

i miss your hair long! my shoulders are broad & i dislike change!

i want to be a painter
who lives in an orca's mouth
i'll dip my brush through the blowhole

yellow equals subtraction! hickeys yellow at the end! magenta
me under a bridge again!

i am always ready for the next kiss! i crescent back for a third
before the first has ended!

daytime moons are the perfect result of industrial revolution
roust early & impersonate bronze!

we don't hunt for geodes! we used to hunt for geodes!

thank gravity for shadows! i begin at your feet!

a greenhouse is a lighthouse! for anything that breathes!

how do i accuse you of forgetting! say, "love, why don't we have the same nightmares!"

when i hold you i also remember you! your scent! the limn of venus-dust on a spacesuit! you turn each moment into the last one

how to get closer than a fingerprint! deeper than goodnight!

we have to cauterize the skyline

we have to suture the rain

self-portrait as angel baby

i must be little
or young to keep my name. i was told
this once, by a woman my mother
would hate, in a place softer
than swampland. in alberta, the animals
linger eye-level along the walls,
decapitated –

the men i know leech hunting dogs
on what they care to keep. i am a girl & a too tight
phylactery. lost teeth or bloodspill
these are the same: i go crying
to closed arms.

i do not understand these new loves:
to hang lanterns
from the antlers of the living, to divide the numbers
by every abuse they remember.

      i am predated
      & i am predated. on the prairies,
      a girl can run for hours
      & still

many mornings i fill
whatever vessel will surround me. many mornings this defines
my limits. waking up i cannot open my eyes or i am closer
to death than kittenhood.

with each smalling
i disembody, enhance. a bunny must be little
or young to keep its name. yet what is tiny
can be replaced. i am so sweet
i have blood all over; a viscera
of rabbit, a miniature of the great
someday.

       i left my throat
       in alberta.
             a pink snowglobe, the moon.

fourteen forms of imprinting

1
any creature who arrives before all others
named mother for lack of parents
songbirds follow microlight
aircraft to learn
aviation

2
trust as a collection of traits:
    those eyes;
    a city-face, best seen reflected;
    corrosiveness;
contagious insomnia;
    those eyes –

3
univocity of scent
possible gunpowder possible firework

4
ducklings as contrails to fawns

5
to willingly become jetsam
to accept orbit as purpose
to halo to halo to halo
to allow the intolerable

6
how the inflicting thing
remains unbruised
while a thigh blueblacks,
or a moonlike cheek

7
self-metonymy, alight & migratory,
to a hot air balloon father

8
a craving for repetition

9
as far back as pre-birth
a craving that burns through
no & no & no

10
a worship known as primacy; peeling
& boiling the egg from inside out

11
fawns as contrails to ducklings

12
hunting inverted, sideways –
target as predator as kin

13
those eyes

14
the purple fist, the ulcer tongue,
the eyes, the eyes,
the enamel mouth, the animal –

self-portrait in leo

o i am ravenous.

as a sea urchin
i'd have who i belong to
right in my name.

my cheeks are so filthy i'm somebody's
lost baby: fingers salty
with silence, chest flat
with unlovability.

at low tide, even the sea.

as an urchin i would beg
for a safehouse,
a mother, a map
with fewer hydras –

one of five heads always
left out of the kisses.

     as an urchin
     i'd have jester dreams
     by my mimed self:
        my palace! mine!

o to be held by narrow
elbows on all sides.

even the sea leaves me.

chicago laundry

slim and strong as a samurai, you wash socks in our frequently
broken kitchen sink. you say, as if citing the weather, *murder
rate escalating – must be the summer heat.* i hold your hips
between my hands. you feel so narrow and brief, i ache when i
don't touch you. chicago is capital city for murder and stand-up
comedy, a juxtaposition too bright to look at. murder rate rising
means there are fewer people to watch it rise. i say, *why would
anyone exert themself to murder in july?*

we have breakfast for dinner over the chicago tribune:
clementines in tissue paper, tea, eggs, toast. it's july so
every glance feels like waking up; it's july so sunset is the
only appropriate attire. this heat wave spangles bridges and
doorsteps and corpses in landfills and god's sweaty toes and
late evening traffic. rush hour at all hours, rats in the walls, a
cockroach moon. the world wants to end and i don't know how
to end it. in black-and-white, every article reads like a ransom
note, your coffee rings brown cuffs on the tablecloth. cops and
dead men; serial killers and dead women.

the city is asking for a place to stay, so i open all our windows,
laundry turning humid on balcony railings, and kiss you how
the noon sun kisses dials. at night, making love, we whisper
about conspiracy theories, hate crimes, the word *sanctuary.*

here, take this: my body, amber shadow cast over your skin –
chalk outline. i want you held inside me. *now i'm thirsty, are
you thirsty, darling? now i am thirsty.*

let's make a pact, a proposal: oh, i want to feel safe.
   someday we've got to threaten this city;
   someday we've got to matter here.

new laws of falconry

try to reverse war without finding raw.
try to have a hobby that isn't somehow war
or improv
or stretching a mangled fist.

imagine this:
you make a living naming birds
which already exist & are too large to be pinned in boxes.

imagine, worse:
you make a living naming nothings
& don't know how you're alive.

anyway, you masturbate too much to have a left hand, to throw
darts.

the upstairs neighbours roll a rubber ball across what you call
ceiling.
or too many intruder feet
or one huge millipede.

as your mother said:
in this quicksand, you're an eel. you didn't know
what she meant then.

anyway, war:
there are hawks bjorning.
there's the gun, the checkered flag, the white flag
censored.

how do you go so fast you sound like a ball.
how do you bleed the hurriedness of rubber from yourself.
these are thoughts you have in bed because you are a fool.
these are thoughts you have sideways with your fingers inside
yourself
as such algophobia.

drinking nuclear lemonade, you dissolve.
no battle, just a world of solutes.
then you & everyone are sugar. the quail & ptarmigan turn to
ash.

you self-hunt in preparation –
take the gun out of the fridge
& clean it.

though why clean it.
& why not fuck yourself.
& why sweep the floor for the visiting king.

there are free concerts all summer. there's a sauna & a steam
room & a pool
so you come out the same as you went in. find your temple
again shot to pieces. it's fragment season.

this year,
a zodiac for bloodletting.
you've heard this all before.

self-portrait in virgo

i know blame.

i have the eye
of an omnivore – i look up
when it rains.

an owl's neck can turn forever without breaking.

    i used to believe
    so much.

windup baby mouse

i am the only mouselet
with no hunger no heritage no labyrinths
perfect & pinkless & crafted.

do i wind up at the joints
or from the back – one key or three hundred & sixty
i am tiny
& belaboured with tasks.

in nirvana, a sewer of lifeboats,
    fledermaus
    fledermaus –
rats have their own many-armed eyeless
god but i know none of his names.

    i must be strong
    because i cannot
    be prey.
    i must be
    come strong because i can
    not –

to a microscope i amphigory. i have no gore only purposes.
to nothing do i baby. i baby to nothing. babies outré from an
    embryo.

no, no, no.

hello
from vermin innocence. hello
from windup baby.

veruca salt at the triangle shirtwaist factory

day one & the want   becomes need

outside, the moon   in mercury paint

but there are garments   to gild out of sugar

                                            garments heavy on the gills

                                            & thread of wildfire

daily the grief, the grief   the gears unturning

daily the v. salt   to the lungs

we are a silo

we are a silo   we are assailed

all our unmets   float   in the air as motes

& when this fact   ory ruins me

        still i am a childlike   wonder

        empty hands beg

        of gods & mothers   fathers & monsters

we, the workers
deliver our gold
en birds of flame
even as they peck
our selves to death

until we drift
                together

                together as ash in air
                                so, so far above

self-portrait in libra

my neighbours' snails seem less in need of empathy
or i cannot crush them

the reluctant way water drips from the branch — like an
afterthought
is my greatest fear

i would rather fall heavenward
than be caught empty-handed

all my lovers have filleted me in the community garden
on the way home from the bar
    i just want to try it once
    i'd say as if they were the first
    past their shoulders overlooked
    those shuttered orange windows – that home
    for protagonists

my favorite video of me is the one where i'm flirting with the
cameraman
the light is purple
the light is flirting too

when i was little i thought hurricanes were hungry
& they needed me to live
    & um i still do

what's the point of anything with limits
wish i'd been a latchkey kid
or broken a bone. at least once i should've taken
plan b in high school. why even keep
an unshared memory?

how i look holding a clementine

then peeled awake & pressed into the day
sometimes i get so angry i eat my fingers joint by joint
sometimes i exigent into the pulp

the first time i gave top in the calgary airport i went down at
sunrise
right after my plane landed & when i came up the sky was
sunset
like a grapefruit candle & with one lung
i couldn't breathe for a week

so hey.
i do think i am beautiful
but it's a pyrrhic beauty

you've never loved anyone until you love me
sorta scene

when someone leaves me again i'm like
ok shut up
    & in a way they do

    i leave my sheets to dry under the wet moon

        how a moth vanishes in a sprig of light –
        believing that it too is something to see by –

            that is my greatest fear

wisdom tooth blues

you have the same mating call as death & you're both
hitchhikers. this goldenrod
road a moat. a separation from home, even as it leads there.

i've been that girl in the driver's seat,
with a cricket in her ear canal. i've had antlers
& horns, all types of exposed bone except those
that speak to weakness.

you brush your teeth more often than the shadows shift.
bringing, everywhere, this toad
body, this slug tongue: guts, gullet, gimlets. i recall your old
songs, that keening to filth,
or to belonging. a red mud that makes amphibians
indistinguishable.

what's a pearl necklace? polishable, always? not strong enough
to suspend a talisman, an anvil.

if you were a serpent you'd slither
into your ex-loves' mouths. down past the uvula. don't say
you wouldn't. i've been in their mouths,
i've been death once. so i know.

a pearl necklace is heaven on gums. a pearl necklace is what
you'd choke on
if you listened harder to your own cries; down your throat
or around.

where along the highway
can you ensure cleanliness. sunset & sunrise
seem identical: wet laundry
unseparated, the reds turned pink, the blues.

i'm telling you the soul
in all its parts is human
except one. was it the extra gland,
the lack of voicebox? what's a pearl necklace?
if broken,
          a path?

self-portrait in scorpio

since i was little the men have called me
hospital bait; touch me & i'll frostbite
ur extremities.

when i am hungry i just
devour.

i couldn't stand to be more delicate.

i used to get turned inside out
& shaken for pennies.

have u ever been loved
because u are easy?

on my tiptoes i can almost reach
what i can almost reach.

can u not say
destroy
like it's always a bad word.

the men used to gossip
it's not fun if she wants it.

but i want them all dead
& that's so wonderful.

wait

can u not beg
as if it'll get u forgiven?

sell an organ. shed
ur name.

i've often been just pretty
enough to eat. how do u think
i feel?

foodchain
all disarrayed
at my feet.

keep asking for what i cannot see
& i'll say make me
make me
make me.

cumslut

i need a word to search for porn. of a girl who subsists on the thrust of her six male roommates. of course this is a sitcom about found family. but how to get the trajectories? to assert that she is a nonentity & essential to the home? she has the girl-next-door storyline, gem earrings & blue jeans, likeable tendencies; she's known all these boys for life. as they cook dinner/play video games – they summon her with the tender threat of belonging. they have made her a pixie by giving her a true & secret name. the name with which they call her home when she's off biking, her keyhole thighs raised from the seat. they require her in order to feel holy. all she has to say to ask for praise is that it makes her finish. for yes, they want her ended. really what is the term for that fetish? to always be surrounded? to be moon-splashed in touch like drowning? her eyes, shiny enough to swallow a sunset. her body as iconic as the heron etched on the back of a coin. at the sight of a bough storm-thrown through the ceiling, she opens enormous with whimsy, an aperture in her plexus. no matter what the collision she cannot resist. seven steps from apollo 11 she would let aldrin jetsam the mouth & armstrong jetsam the back. the distant world's news would know her as darksider. all summer the pretty girls would wear torn space suits & blow their skulls open. then i would be the girl & she would be me. the mind-body problem would solve via pert tits: mind is surprise! ghost gargles machine. together we form the tangle at the center of the rat king. through us the rats must never leave each other. our collarbones, gutters – for dna we now own. these boys made ours just slightly less than we are theirs. we guzzle pie from neighbor windows. we awaken at the feet of quilts as rescue pets & do not know euthanasia besides that it sounds like a word for joy. in my porn the same six boys who made us get to finish us, & we are forever no more than a hand away –

if i wanted an explosion in my hands

i would change my lightbulbs   instead my house
all dark like a horror movie   at least if i lived in a glass place
with one spherical wall? i would be moth girl   i would die when opened
the joke is how many space cadets   to change a lightbulb   then they unscrew
their helmets   & show their brains to space   all my coins are star-shaped
my body is bald all over for kisses   the joke is how many pretty girls
the joke is i hold my hands out but nobody gives me   coffins or vending machines
or these oblong boxes   bright inside   fridges & tanning beds
& the box for the bad kittens   i would like to join them if we go swimming
at least the river ends in a rainbow & behind   every waterfall a gnome-hole
so i've heard   although: can't believe everything you've gnome-holed
me & everyone i know   have our hands up empty   undoing
palms at the sky with the fingers like firepits in circles   maybe a coconut falling
will blackout us from too high above   deadtime for good –
for good?   for good   how bad can a kitten be
can't discover gravity   & stay alive – well maybe   but become parasite
opposite of sightline   the joke is a cavern   the joke is a sundress   the joke
is gargoyle   the joke is good is illuminous   is tangible   is normalcy
akin to narwhal is spinning   is solar flare   is steeple   is toll taker   tell me
the joke & i'll say what it is

self-portrait of the obsessive compulsive
in isolation

i should like to be dismantled. in the light. a white onion.
my skull still soft. the apartment half-moved-out.

my roommate   an archer   opens the tight-
lidded jars   her hands
          making elf doors.

the parks & parking lots   as mingling places are closed.
no perks! no mangle!

everytime i'm free   i think oh i hope

i will yank the cityscape inside out
by the skyscraper. maybe a bank-burning. instead usually
i end up in the bike shed
touching my breasts.

suffer wallpaper. suffer a bowl of grapes. suffer a grass-blower
(machine
that blows the grass around).

earlier much earlier
i got on his hips on the bedroom carpet & we transferred
bruises
between us & i said, this is how i am drunk, & i meant it
exponentially. this is the only way
he stays: by disaster. he or she
or he or whoever.

sex is love
for the object impermanent but
do not eat the yellow plastic.

& in my nervous
system all the ants
communicate their passage through jazz –

why write a song if it is not also a threat. i.e. veins
that dream of outside. i.e. pollen season.

suffer the blown-glass ozone. i still worry when i place stickers
though on my shoulder
blades the tattoos remember:
            need need
need need.

before the outbreak my shrink
asked if i had ever been masticated
as a child & i said
haha.   how would i know.

i forget & forget. as a toddler
i wore an eyepatch & cried constantly
for a monocle to match.

fact: peanut oil
makes cyanide act faster   so when i eat pb with apple
slices
i am careful about the seeds
usually

i end the year
before its end. all i have to say is
no more! i make frayed ends
before the real end so i never have to be

all year my throat says uh oh
the new number is coming –

i am a girl & i am trying. if i could swallow me, i would!
okay?   i've tried!

i knead bread too hard to be a lover anymore. Still
i would let any pretty fuck
in nail polish hit me with a cement truck   just to see
the young magenta of my insides   still sometimes
i practice narcissism at the obsidian alter   where
my face but dark & shiny!

                    see? what is lovelier than making the arrow
                    disappear & change at once?

confession.
at the dentist
i always want to smuggle the pink & teal hygienists
home in my root canal. if i am being pieced together
why start at the tooth. incised, i bet
the belly of a great white
would look like cut-up pear.

i shouldn't quit my shrink. play spin the bottle
in the dark alone. i shouldn't take up hemophilia. or six fake
lives.

incarnation & incarceration –   perhaps the same
in the insect farm?

i write threats
to myself
on the bedframe to keep time. time is what i am keeping for
later.

this is the only way i remain: by disaster.

nobody cums rat poison anymore

do they want us to starve. i did a bad thing;
i wore a bad thing's coat. to wash everything at once
requires nakedness. so you stand by the washing machine
& i kneel in front of the rinse cycle.
i am trying to perform unloving; a monologue, the opposite
of a blow job. i flinch at the name
birthmark.

& how do you define clean? as waterboarding
a girl in the world's longest river
until she too becomes either amazon
or alligator? does clean
mean all my ex-lovers are selkies
& i owe them their sweaters back? i throw patrick's housekeys
in a wishing well,   lose jason's mitten
in a cursed swamp,   sell ella's false eyelashes
to malevolent fairies as prosthetic wings.

i am more attainable than any other object
because i have desires. i am a slut, or i wear a slut's
nothingness. maybe if i turn enough other mouths inside out
you will become negative space.

rinsecycle rinsecycle, maybe i will move with water
in order to evaporate.
liquid, i will have no hands for it. let me give nixies UTIs. or
instead of all this,
why don't we hide in the dryer
& suffocate like kids?

please hold me like a fleet of piranhas!
please love me like i'll return
infinity times! nobody cums barbed wire
anymore. it's like they want me intact!
if love doesn't kill me something worse than love will.
what's better? i wish i could want you less than you want me
but a wish is a want
is a havoc is a portuguese man-of-war.

come dawn
there's more left than i'd expect: lint, the smell of lemon,
one of your socks. still,
you don't cum acid rain anymore –
are you trying to knock me up? i am redunding the same ideas
with different intonations. sure, the shape of an umbrella
outlines the eightfold path to rainclouds. sure,
you leave every room like someone without fingerprints, like a
chess player:
touch-move, touch-take. but if redemption is newness then
where
is the newness in that?

that summer i thought i was gautama buddha

i knew the presumptiveness but the way my limbs hurt & the way
i fluctuated from nothing to gluttony to garish
forgetting – unsure who i last touched & why. an anger started
in my thighs
but i kept it there. it was the summer the man who believed
hemingway became   kurt cobain   became him
made me suck him almost all the way off
in a movie theatre stairwell. i'd spend 35
dollars at a time on quarters. my mother said
baby where'd you put all my combs? my mother said
baby what do you deserve? all summer
i fermented under the grape trees, figured
that meant progression, a claw
into the next life. every new meal
like a bruise, undoable. maybe i'll never tell my mother
what happens in the real world. i nonattached
from consequences, it was easier to be someone
long-dead, or long-existed, but grapes
don't grow on trees, i know. imagine saying: "i checked –
you are perfect." maybe i needed
david bowie, hot rain, banana bread,
finger tattoos, diet pepsi, a shaved head,
second base, a meteor shower
behind 7-eleven, david bowie in real life,
music in reverse, a handshake, a job at the post office, hide 'n' seek
with somebody's brother, new underwear, green eyes,
a charity case, a lawsuit, a coma, a win, a long run
in flip flops, david bowie's
head on a platter. maybe

there were too many corners
in too many rooms. my rage monsooned
into every flesh i had. i saw more than six
awfuls & that alone could be a sin. but my mother already
knows
what the world does & grapes
do grow on trees.

states of matter

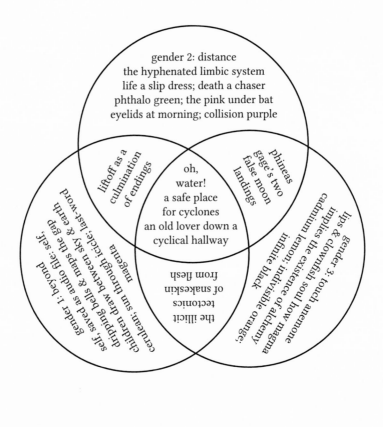

gender 2: distance
the hyphenated limbic system
life a slip dress; death a chaser
phthalo green; the pink under bat
eyelids at morning; collision purple

liftoff as a culmination of endings

phineas gage's two false moon landings

oh,
water!
a safe place
for cyclones
an old lover down a
cyclical hallway

the illicit tectonics of snakeskin from flesh

gender 1: beyond self, saved as audio file; self, dripping bells & maps the gap children draw between sky & earth cerulean; sun through icicle; last-word magenta

gender 3: touch anemone implies the existence of alchemy cadmium lemon; indivisible black lips & clownfish soul how infinite; black magma anemone; indivisible orange;

man must destroy in himself the desire to feel pleasure

what is the point of a hand
job. man hands
are for scraping. as a woman i writhe, & my mattress stains tell me
i fall in love faster than i hold –   our bodies
roll up in kites & so can't fly. if women are nights, men
are knights. manhood begins
in whatever you can quell.   let's split a razor & see
who comes away smooth. delicacy
trumps fragility anyday, but still scythe off your arm
hairs as soon as they rise. me i crave
any holiday.   shouldn't you be out
breaking strange bones? if you say
let's be blood brothers
you mean let's drink broth together
until we die without teeth. what i crave i'll have:
fanta in the stream, bare chest on the balcony. surrendering
virginity to the lake & taking it back,
wringing it out in a shining
sheet of magenta & daybreak. slick
as new.
        for you:
sword over sugar, stoicism over sex. come home
with your shield or
as i am:
        wings spread on shoulder
        blades, fighting
        for the cervix of god.

laika of cop-killing

"i just killed a cop now i'm horny." — JPEGMafia

"Negro Matapacos ('Black Cop-Killer') was a famous stray dog from
the streets of Santiago who joined student protests across the city from
2010, and in particular during the 2011 movement for free education.
Negro Matapacos was then seen regularly at every demonstration,
defying tear gas and water cannons and always barking at or attacking
only the riot police, and never any students or rioters. He subsequently
continued to appear sporadically at future demonstrations, and hung
out on university campuses, becoming beloved to student and radical
movements as a symbol of resistance to violent authority." — *Working
Class History* podcast, on Chile's "riot dog"

you just killed a cop now you're hungry. with cop guts you craft
a cat's cradle that rocks you to praxidike. you win the space race
of entrails. with blooded tongue you lick no hand with a ring.

kiss only the unmarred hand.

now you determine the sacrifices to science. breathe orbital
        jupiter. meteoroid
the state's dominance: from unreachable rock to mere streak of
        skylight. riot shield
as your blooded tongue. you strum a mayan downpour. riot
        shield as oxymoron

but not if riot is shield.

*it is deeply regrettable. through this mission this was understood:
it's regrettable. not enough could be learned from that voyage
to justify the death of a dog.*

so spaceflight for doglife is incommensurate. what about city on
    fire, sleep-faced
children, these boys still growing into their eyes, all taxonomies
    of motherhood?
you ask in the common language so you cannot be unheard;
    you ask in a tooth translation:

new latin for men with grenades.

there's the catch: only way to stop a gun. now you determine
    the sacrifice state.
alongside your pink rain, no fasces sprout. reflected on jupiter,
    a future: the city
holds its own sans siege & starvation. for the pack, sometimes
    you must gaur boar –

crucial boar eclipse on a roasting spit.

sometimes boar dinner & boar breakfast, boar afterthought &
    boar sandwich,
boar agriculture & boar ammonia, boar suffer & boar soupstock,
    boar bastard
& boar grenadine, boar accident & boar applesauce. now you
    determine the safety.

on praxidike it's haven.

it's red in the right way. tiger lilies & anemones nourished on
    enforcer flesh.
sycamores decade through policia ribcagia. the pups here are
    reared to mama
each other & no one dies in the sputnik of must. under a
    bonemeal canopy,

    an extra terrestria.
    what stops a gun
    but a good dog
    in the bad past.

self-portrait in sagittarius

in all my past lives i was bait.   still i bleed from both ends
like a trapped rat. the question then is how to stop. whatever i do,
i breed obsession. hence the polaroids hanged like rosemary
over the stove – easily the photos cook into oil spills of colour. hence
the way i memorize the lifelines of a one-night stand. there's a lot to see again,
so i exit   each life as quickly as i can.   i've been a fainting goat, a canary.
i slip out through the cat flap & a hawk takes me hunting.   then i see the world from above
through predator eyes.   when i'm eaten i render the hawk into me –
my heart all DDT.   next   i'm yellow striped & smell of honey
& anyone who follows   in my footsteps   has to dance.

after a one-night stand with Myself
i ask Myself to stay the night

i know she wants me
by her side in sleep. i do not really   ask   her to stay,
only imply she is invited. i speak
our language. now i understand why no one wants me
to hickey them over the collar & on the wrist, all these visible
marks of myself. Myself
touches me as if she is an endangered species of jungle cat
that craves everyone it sees. we kneel & braid each other's
hair from the front, reach over shoulder, pull from the nape.
though we reflect one another
i am jealous of Myself, the perfect way she uses her fingers.
Myself can finish me
so much faster than i can; she sees in me
a target. i do not envy that all her kisses
are anxious with farewell. not everyone understands
how to care for endangered predators. even knowing how
much she needs,
i want Myself to post a photo of us together, though we only
just met –
hours earlier at a bus station. in the blue of a rain-smeared
window
she appeared. i wish Myself would forgive me,
without my having to ask, for sleeping with yet another friend
who has broken the heart
of someone i love. i do it all the time. we love to fuck
heartbreakers
because it makes us feel intact. we can look each other
in the heartbreaking smile & not diminish. yet i know
that after Myself leaves, i will fall asleep on only half the
mattress. she will decide to leave –
            but first we go to bed again

to prove that we are irresistible. both of us are willing
to wear the 8-inch purple cock
to make it easier, but really
we would each rather be the princess of lollipops, purple
tongues & purple
thumbs & purple knees. we both hate self-
pleasure, because what, do we not care
about the nuclear holocaust & the famine in that other country?
but we both love to watch it happen so why the fuck
do we get off. from the back i see Myself as if
in a hairdresser's mirror, same dainty
broad body. the calves strain under oceanic tattoos & the waist
is perhaps the parabola of time. we breathe   in
spaces between:
I   I   I   therefore?   after,
we twine each other like a lemon grove, as if
to remain. but
Myself chooses cab fare
from the dresser & kisses me
on my hip-soft cheek.
when my lower lip quivers it means my mouth needs filling.
we've been like this since forever.
she puts her thumbs over my eyelids
& swipes the tears away. even she does not stay
the night. until the taxi leaves view i hug
the doorframe in a borrowed shirt & hope
she's going home to no one.

neptune in capricorn

the math works.

i spend sixty
percent of my life planning the other sixty.

every time i see the moon i'm at the bottom of a well again.

thrice a day i pray to geppetto.
tongue on my pulse.

i am to camera girl as centaur is to capture.

my toxic trait is i cannot pass a CAPTCHA.

at least i have the tenderest cunt.

behind the 7/11 i vape a UFO language.
i bite my nails & everyone knows
i am queer.

in a million years
the archeologists will sort through the gumball machines
at the mall & say
look at all this worship.

cumslut ii

      what am i if not
spitroasted in a mosh pit? am i god's lesser daughter,
grown in heat? doing third base at calgary stampede,
i think my arms would no longer yearn to fall off from grief.
within my many throats i find
foreign earrings. at any unidentified object
      i fear i am

unfaithful to myself. i would like to reach into the flesh exactly
between my true love's hips & pull from within her a tangle of
multicolored light. instead
each stranger a stack of bodies in a trench coat – familiar
as sunday morning animation, & as morbid. nothing allures like
the space
behind a drifting curtain, the colour blue in mid-july. the mosaics
seem like false tunnels lately: cartoonish to enter –

      as am i.

i wake up in the girlfriend hour, my girlfriend leaves dropping
off from heaviness –
so easily i am overwatered. the first time
a popstar touched my wrist i left that spot dry for a week. i
scrubbed around it
like a fresh wound so it seemed to glow
yet by the seventh day i woke up filthy. once, a lover told me
nobody kisses like you do, you make it different –
& i put that sentence in a locket so if i ever hanged
upside down those words would stay. for new year's eve i said
i'd become a slut for endings, so i tried to unknow his name. by new
year's day i dislocated my arms from their sockets so i'd have
two extra holes –

i am a polly pocket doll! in the hot wet mouth! of a
universe that's already
swallowed my shoes!

as a child i could not sleep until i'd whispered,
under my covers, to my soft-skulled body:
>i love you
>i you love
>i you love
>owe you love
>o, you love
>o, you, love.

from the temporary back of my head would osmosis
all this surfeit heartbeat, so much
i could not sleep. without object permanence it was still so easy
to believe in any beautiful thought. without object permanence
i was the object,
the beautiful thought. with object permanence, what am i if not
pitted in a concert hall? what am i if not
the space between bodies? what am i when i
>am not looking?

y2k for final girls

often, a twin appears to you.   you each hold a grapefruit to compare
their weight.   under the pool it seems you come from a blue world. in the nightclubs
& afterparties you're lit blue too   like a study in survival. it's almost tomorrow
always. no wonder you're sad. animals test   your every breath.   cry off mascara
& you waste a bunny death.   day by day you get sicklier & more depraved
to camouflage with the ghost women under your bed.   you walk into rooms
& walk through yourself.   your first memory is crawling from the lake & trading
your pelt for legs. or, first memory: freaky friday
with whom you could have been.   into another life?
is there a stranger in here,   don't you want to be dazzled
          or is your house on fire?   often, your twin a mirror
who uncraves your life. often, your twin a sundial, a stereotype, a phonograph cylinder,
a shadowbox,   a slow dance,   a consequence. often, your twin
the century you do not save.   every moment a brutal doppelganger
of the last. aren't there 10 types of people in the world – those who   each other
& those who gemini?   so easily you're the last two girls on earth, your hands blue
with change, your souls stained with each other. it's just safety   to turn ghost.
how do you work when you do not yet know   how the world will end?

self-portrait in aquarius

careful.

everywhere we step,
spring worms.

i say this a lot –
in the yellow supermarket;
risky naps under the coconut trees;
at dusk in the desert –
but it's not about death.

that's only the umbrella.

all year in cardigans
i wait for fall.

a lot of love is just guessing
at how to craft joy. simultaneously i climb down
both sleeves
to find the heartbeat.

but what a way to slice in half:
splitting
into droplets.

the best thing about me

i am a plover that feeds off crocodile teeth.
    the crocodile dies but i do not.
        i shelter in the jawbones.
            the scales bleach to nothing.
                i bring life to a lifeless mouth.

when i'm in danger it's like two strangers trying to pass
in the hallway.
i bet you will not eat me – oh, my shadow isn't touching you.

god wants me dead so bad he breaks his first sweat.
he sends tall men whose thumbs taste of blood.

i am raze-bait,
incorrigible & wire boned.

they taste more of blood when i am done!

look away & i become a baby turtle
split from birth & bound for ocean.
the birds harbour a divine hunger.

always i crawl toward the reflection of light.

yes, i am edible

yes, i am edible!

but
　　　i dare you i dare you i dare you i dare you i dare you
　　　i dare you i dare you i dare you i dare you i dare you
　　　i dare you i dear you i scare you i dire you i dare you
　　　i dare you i damn you i scry you i scorn you i care you
　　　i dare you i dare you i dare you i dare you i dare you

image of the prince's castle
with dying deer in foreground

isn't it supposed to be the prince who stoics the ache, his jesters
slapping his capable back,
until a new girl arrives to congruent the last: a girl in a gray
sundress who heals his head
against her lap.

throughout the castle the end tables i invert to spill tureens of
meat soup across ivory rooms.
sundays i stand barefoot on the grounds; a girl, a gray sundress,
tightening the stoic at the back
of my throat.

i have yet to learn the words for this loss but please there must
be words. until then is it alright?
is it alright to turn the half-broken neck to watch the castle
burning? the red across the lawn used
to belong to me.

the mud is a mud of my insides. if castles exist to spite gravity
then courage
is also a crater. i am exhausted of the prince
transforming peasant women into his own hands, hoarding
village herbs in his mouth.

why make handmaids of the youngest serfs. why hunt for a
new beast to despise.

     orpheus
     in looking back committed a violence. love her better.

the prince demands:

a well at the base of the stairs, a menagerie of lingerie, iron
bars, climbing ivy, an alibi, buckshot,
servants, "servants," traps sprung by only the lightest footsteps.
is that a story? there's conflict,
& creation, & me on the lawn, split apart into too many selves,
looking back.

looking back with no choice but to look back, the spine
desecrated, the dappled hide
against the grass, pale underbelly bleached with viscera. here
my passage, secret, here my
servitude, i'm the deer, i'm the girl, i'm the castle, i'm
everywhere now.

look, look:

i bet the bullet will be named not for who fired it
        but for what it kills.

self-portrait in pisces

to tear apart – i am as easy as an apple.

i'm worried my favorite ex will sleep with my other favorite ex
& then i'll be a landfill.

at that party i was such a pisces.

night swimming in the fountain gave me flu & i ripped my blue
dress, the one that barely comes past the ass so there's almost
nothing to rip.

if a hemline goes past the knees i get uni-knee
& i get mud stains if a skinny boy wears a big green sweater
& i like him too much
which is usually.

i'm gonna get a tattoo of everything that happened this summer
so i don't forget.

a rope swing on my spine dances when i do. spiked cocoas in
july, blood moon.

kissing me is mostly
getting given back.

i'm worried i'm nobody's favorite ex.

i'm worried about purgatory. that there's a party going on
without me.

i'm worried when i'm in halves i won't get to keep one.

actually babylon of the whore

is the correct possessive. it is the season
of the hive. by streets we speak of saffron
rivers. by homes we speak of the only places
we will not set on fire. the sole antidote
we can imagine for the current climate
is an apocalypse for its rulers. we need riot
or the meek will inherit. meek of heart & meek
of joy. when dragonflies mate they rat-king,
centrifugal in the skies. the face of an ancient
angel is a honeycomb of eyes, while the night
is a cornucopia of spiders. what we mean is:
fellowship in strangeness. none of us could
ever be dogs. why eat what is your own. be
it tail or be it bitch. the real ouroboros we met
in a marketplace, she was a honduran grandmother
gifting oranges infinitely. god is just a tall boy
who offers us nothing. god is the heartbreaker
but never the harlot. the best aspect of outer space
lies in its premise: slut-land of sunsets. elsewhere,
where the sweethearts thrum.

no, fuck the possessive. share the city among angels.
why aren't they god.

why aren't they god.

two rats living in a raccoon's corpse discuss structural brutalism

rat 1:
it is so red in here
what is a lobster

rat 2:
like lobster red
i lived in one once
no not in the water
just in the body
on the shore.

where does this end?
at the ribs?
how much is everywhere –

i guess it spills everywhere.
well it makes a mess.
it's all monolith.

then how does it end.
oh, that can stay.

there's ligament in your teeth.

i feel like a hermit crab.
consuming our home.

cause of the sand?
they don't do that.

wouldn't they, if –
home turns into us.
home rots anyway.

well that's no safety.

well that's no safety.

no, no safety.

self-portrait in aries

i have been so alive.

in an open shirt i set mint sprigs on fire.

we brush each other's teeth in the speckled mirror.

my limbs made yours in watercolor.

you can bow a cherry stem with your tongue;

i can keep a chick alive in the slickness of my cheek.

yes, i am a pet for care.

little body all skeletal with rain.

it's so easy not to break me once you know that i am breakable.

you were hungry.

i was hungry.

& the thing to eat was in me.

speeeeeeeeed

i get it, quicks.

paint my nails & i won't bite them
is a husbands' tale. i still bite.

i don't ask for girlfriend rights
on the third date anymore
but i still put out after two shrimp & a cider.

not everything's about me but
isn't it though? it's my life, my fast
& brutal touch.

i'm a kind learner. i get it already.

can't we just hold hands
& walk between cars.

can't we

love store

i want to make love but you take me to the love store. the walls
are sunset without the pinks. you pick up items resembling
honeydew, lace baby socks, cherry-red ball gags, & put them
back down. your long hands are aphrodisiacs. sometimes i feel
like medusa: victim of mirrors, thoughts full of snake tails. i say,
where do you think she put the shed skin every month? but your
mouth is full of free samples. i think medusa let her snakes eat
for her. not a single bite would cross her lips. i bet she caught
mice for them in the least cruel traps she knew. i want to make
love but you say, *we have love at home.* the love at home has
freezer burn & tastes of tupperware. *it's not right to waste good
love,* you say, buttoning your shirt up to your chin like some
lawyer's son. a radio behind the unmanned desk plays a jazz
song that reminds me of a different lover, the smell of basement
& of thighs.

at the back of the store, animals fracked into obsolescence live
their little half-lives: mammoths and carrier pigeons in dim
tanks all backlit. they are translucent with forgottenness &
they watch us as lost pennies do. you enter the backroom – for
employees only – & i follow through these stage curtains. from
above, among storage, drops a Titanoboa, open mouth large
enough to swallow you whole. the fangs are blue with wanting.
its sound is the hiss of air escaping from air. it exists mostly in
extinction – with love & without heart – & so you walk right
through it: a second curtain, a phantom limb born torsoless.
you: as if it is nothing to walk through what once had a life
larger than your own.

i close my eyes when i pass the Titanoboa. when i was younger
& still learning to be bloodless at least once a month, i would
sometimes put the tortoiseshell handle of a hairbrush inside me.
i thought, then, i could summon care by pretending i did not
want it. now, medusa: i'm rebirthed through destruction.

in the backroom you hold me by my miniature parts – my
wrists, my neck, my ears – & slide unbought earrings into
places i have no holes. your hope cannot help but puncture.
i want to make love but my hair is too sacred. if i do not kiss
you in the love store, am i the thief of love? into my endless
collarbone, you whisper all the ways you want to shoplift from
me. you want to take my baby socks, my ballgags. i want to
make love but i've shed it all for you.

self-portrait in taurus

the hunger strike lasted for a day.
guess i'm irresistible.

hello encyclopedia –
how do i wake up ruthless.

when i kiss the king's ring
i'm a buck-tooth guillotine.

every day since the revolution
i've tried to be better.

my dress undid in the riot &
i didn't even try to fix it.

audition for Survivor,
ending in hummingbirds

because i have my father's shoulders
    & birthing hips

because in the winter i am abstinent of syrup, honey, oil, wine,
    butter, flower,
    all the good quilts

because i'd fit in a margherita glass

because i'd do anyone to pixelate
    & small

because i am so hungry i inside out

because i can say no forever

        because i have my father's sobriety
           & unbirthing lips

        because in the summer i make dirt for dinner

        because i taste only
           of sugar licked from rims

           what if the wings
           what if the fractured wings

        because i am already
           so far above
           drinking ambrosia

so far above &
drinking ambrosia

self-portrait in gemini

the right side of my face is the changeling side;
make my skull a peach pit. make my cheek
the wild thing gorging on it, getting fat
til i can recognize neither pit nor thing.

what graces my mother i disgrace.
i wax into who i am best
with salt on my face, body folded
in a fast-food parking lot.

show me a false positive & i'll read the future
in my own ovaries. or show me a photo
so i know that exactly in the instant of photography, someone
touched me,
someone else loved me. my angle of incidence creates a pool of oil
on the tarmac: a.k.a., my own eyes, a.k.a., refraction.
in eight months it will be summer. in three hours
it will be evening.
this afternoon, i am not the version of myself
that fights a seagull for a french fry.

my flesh does not reflect sunlight.
thirst skins me from the inside;
i cannot complete my gut. winter
chipmunks store chestnuts in my pussy.

animals make animals make
etcetera. reproductive systems
give me trypophobia; holes devour holes.
if i had extra organs i wouldn't share them.

my mother said pregnancy feels
like a surfeit of caviar. she gave birth
only so i would stop kicking.

my abdomen was made for spawn, wasn't it?
& eggs! how do eggs stay calm? under the hull
of the chicken? how to crack, not to shatter?
what a horrible   elliptical body!

history condenses in my funny bone.

what i ruin i ruin
for an ancestor who
had my nose, no plague, nine fingers.

notes & acknowledgements

I am grateful to live, work, and create on unceded Songhees, Esquimalt, and W̱SÁNEĆ land. As all settlers who live on "Canadian" soil should, I hold decolonization as a concrete, urgent tenet by which I try to live my life.

Thank you to the following publications and to their hard-working readers, editors, and staff for the care and consideration:

"self-portrait in gemini" originally appeared in *The Fiddlehead* and *This Side of West.*

"nobody cums rat poison anymore" and "laika of cop-killing" originally appeared in *CV2.*

"nobody cums rat poison anymore" originally appeared in *The Warren Undergraduate Review* and in the 2022 *Best Canadian Poetry* anthology.

"two rats living in a raccoon's corpse discuss structural brutalism" originally appeared in *The Malahat.*

"chicago laundry" originally appeared in *Plenitude.*

"actually babylon of the whore" originally appeared in *PRISM International.*

"self-portrait as angel baby" originally appeared in *Canthius.*

"veruca salt at the triangle shirtwaist factory" appeared online with the Poets Corner Reading Series.

"wisdom tooth blues" appeared in *CAROUSEL.*

The title "man must destroy in himself the desire to feel pleasure" is a reimagining of the Mina Loy quote "woman must destroy in herself the desire to be loved."

The line "but it's a pyrrhic beauty" is borrowed from a conversation with my dear friend Jansen Gibbs.

Thank you to Astra Lund-Phillips and SJ Hawse for their creative input when putting this book together.

So much gratitude to *Homology Lit, The New Twenties, Room, The Newfoundland Arts and Letters Award,* and *Augur* for taking chances on my poems.

Thank you, transcendent Canadian poet LJ Ahenda. This collection does not exist without you. Your care and brilliance make me a better writer and a better person.

Thank you, Alex Kung, for your meticulous and empathetic attention to my poems. Trading work with you is an absolute privilege.

Thank you to my writing mentors for their infinitely valuable advice and support, especially Bill Gaston, Shane Book, Lorna Jackson, and Jay Ruzesky.

Thank you to the poets I already admire and to the poets yet to come.

Thank you to my first-year poetry course classmates at the *qathet* VIU campus for being my first writing group.

Thank you to the following libraries, as well as to the writers I worked with and literary programs and events I attended at them: Vancouver Public Library, Victoria Public Library, Salt Spring Island Public Library, Harmsworth Public Library, A.C. Hunter Library, and University of Victoria Library.

Thank you to Jeremy Luke Hill and Shane Neilson at Gordon Hill Press for all the work, belief, and care that went into this book. I am so grateful for the opportunity to publish with you. Thank you to Brutus O'Gorman for perfectly realizing my cover art dreams.

Thank you to all of my writing partners and first readers for loving me and being loved by me, including: Shaelin Bishop, Kyus Hicks, Kurtis Scriba, Ben Korkola, Max Szredni, Sabrina Li, Ciarán Volke, Rahat Saini, Olivia "Nat" Karpyshyn, Rylan Gladson, Brett Hurley, Dylan Clarke, Maddy Atamanchuk, Emily Pegg, Nathan Hessman, Morgan Cross, Andrew Buckley, Alex Buitenhuis, Julya van der Sloot, and so many others.

Thank you to all my friends, all my confidantes, and all my loves.

Thank you, of course and always, Mum and Dad and Harley. I try to show my gratitude to you in everything I do.

about the artists

Sophie Crocker (they/she) is a queer writer, performer, and editor based on unceded Songhees, Esquimalt and W̱SÁNEĆ land and raised on the traditional territories of the Mi'kmaq and Beothuk Peoples. They hold a BFA in creative writing from University of Victoria. Their poetry and fiction have been published internationally.

Brutus O'Gorman is an artist based in Vancouver. Follow him on Instagram: @left_egg.